Peter Lah S.J.

Talitha Kum
2009-2019

Analysis of the Structure and Activities
of the International Network
of Consecrated Life
Against Trafficking in Persons.
A research report

G&BP

Pontificia Università Gregoriana
Pontificio Istituto Biblico

Faculty of Social Sciences, Pontifical Gregorian University September 2019

Progetto grafico di copertina: Serena Aureli

Impaginazione: Yattagraf srls - Tivoli (RM)

© 2019 Pontificio Istituto Biblico
Gregorian & Biblical Press
Piazza della Pilotta 35, 00187 - Roma
www.gbpress.org - books@biblicum.com

ISBN 978-88-7839-**414**-8

Chiesa e Società 4

PONTIFICIA
UNIVERSITÀ
GREGORIANA

Introduction

Sr. Pat Murray, IBVM
UISG Executive Secretary

This year, 2019, is a special one for Talitha Kum, which is celebrating ten years of action and collaboration against the trafficking of persons, a crime which affects tens of millions of people worldwide. In order to confront well-organized networks of traffickers, religious sisters decided ten years ago to make their own human resources available, including an existing network, in order to create a global response capable of confronting this grave crime. Talitha Kum enables sisters and their collaborators to engage in preventative action, to provide assistance to victims, and to promote different ways of helping the healing process and the reinsertion of victims into work and society.

Talitha Kum is a dynamic worldwide network which is continually changing and growing. The networks are open systems; groups are established, grow in strength and sometimes grow weaker for different reasons. During recent years, the International Union of Superiors General (UISG) has supported the work of Talitha Kum, particularly initiatives in the area of formation and communication. These have been identified as two key elements which need strengthening in order to sustain the work of sisters who are working on the ground against trafficking in persons.

Therefore, Talitha Kum, as a complex and decentralized network, is continually changing. Until now it has not been easy to respond to important questions about its operations, such as: how many individual networks belong to Talitha Kum, who participates in the networks, how many people collaborate with each other, and what types of activities do they undertake? Now finally with this publication it is possible to offer responses to these questions.

This study was born though a collaborative partnership involving Sr. Gabriella Bottani SMC, the Talitha Kum coordinator; Professor

Peter Lah SJ and students from the Department of Social Sciences of the Pontifical Gregorian University and the technical expertise of Dr. Domenico Cosentino. They worked together to create the first database for Talitha Kum, and we owe them a debt of gratitude for this important work.

The first part of the study presents a short history of the birth and growth of Talitha Kum. The second part presents data and comparisons from the census data collected by the networks between 2015 and 2018. The final section presents reports of the various activities undertaken by networks that are members of Talitha Kum.

The publishing of this report is another important step towards strengthening the worldwide efforts of religious sisters and others to confront human trafficking which in the words of Pope Francis is "an open wound on the body of contemporary humanity, a scourge upon the body of Christ... a crime against humanity." This report acknowledges with gratitude the work and commitment of so many who work in quiet and determined ways to prevent, rescue and rehabilitate the many women, men and young people who have been victims of this horrendous crime.

Talitha Kum: the generative beginning

Sr. Gabriella Bottani, SMC
Stefano Volpicelli

The first steps

In many parts of the world, there seems to be no end to grave offences against fundamental human rights, especially the right to life and the right to religious freedom. The tragic phenomenon of human trafficking [...] is but one unsettling example of this.

(Pope Francis, Message for the Celebration of the World Day of Peace 2014).

Since the end of the 1990s, some religious sisters working with women victims of violence or in situations of sexual exploitation, mainly in Europe, came into contact with the painful and violent reality of trafficking in persons. They soon perceived the magnitude and the intricacy of what was happening, and began to dialogue among themselves in order to mobilize more resources, and most of all to make their congregations aware of what was taking place.

The International Union Superiors Generals (UISG), now fully aware of this emerging context, asked the UISG Justice and Peace Commission (JPIC) to organize events to study this growing problem. One such gathering took place in Rome in 1998, with the participation of Sr. Lea Ackermann, MSOLA, who had committed herself to work against human trafficking since 1985 in Kenya. The Anti-Trafficking Working Group (ATWG) of the JPIC Commission was the main outcome of the meeting with Sr. Lea.

In 2001, the ATWG presented the phenomena of human trafficking to over 800 general superiors gathered in Rome for the UISG Plenary. In their final statement, the participants at the UISG Plenary declared:

"We, almost 800 women leaders of one million members of Catholic Religious Institutes throughout the world, publicly declare our determination to work

*in solidarity with one another within our own religious communities and in
the countries in which we are located to address insistently at every level the
abuse and sexual exploitation of women and children with particular attention to the trafficking of women which has become a lucrative multi-national
business."*

Declaration of Women Religious Leaders: UISG Bulletin – Special Number 116)

The commitment publicly manifested in 2001 was confirmed
once again by the Religious Superiors during the 2004 UISG Plenary, thus opening the pathway to stronger inter-congregational collaboration among religious congregations in the field of anti-trafficking.

Since its very beginnings, that collaboration, called Talitha Kum,
has been born through processes of dialogue and discernment carried
on by the Sisters committed on-the-ground together with the leaders
of congregations of Women Religious.

Significant milestones

The following milestones mark the birth and growth of the Talitha Kum Networks:

- 2003: The publication "Trafficking in Women and Children:
  Information and Workshop Kit" developed by the JPIC Commission with the collaboration of *Caritas Internationalis*.
  This tool was translated into at least 7 languages and was
  distributed to religious sisters around the world.
- 2004: In Canada, the Conference of Women Major Superiors of Canada created the "Comité d'action contre la traite
  humaine interne et international" (CATHII); in Australia, a
  group of women congregations founded the "Australian Catholic Religious Against Trafficking in Humans (ACRATH)".
- Again in 2004, a collaborative partnership between UISG and
  IOM (International Organization of Migration) was launched.
  The importance of this project in shaping the identity of Talitha Kum requires a more detailed presentation.

From the training sessions to the foundationn of Talitha Kum

The next important step was the collaboration between the International Union of Superiors General (UISG) and the International Organization of Migration (IOM). The concept, which led to realization of the collaborative project, became a concrete proposal during the international conference "21st Century Slavery: The Human Rights Dimension to Trafficking in Human Beings," held in Rome, 15-16 May, 2002. The conference was organized by members of the Diplomatic Corps accredited to the Holy See, in conjunction with the Pontifical Gregorian University, the Pontifical Council for Justice and Peace, and the Pontifical Council for the Pastoral Care of Migrants and Itinerant People.

During that event, the involvement of religious personnel – and especially of women religious – in carrying out preventative initiatives in relation to vulnerable people, as well as providing assistance to victims, was recognised and praised. Unfortunately, according to the panellists, this active commitment was often undermined by the lack of preparation and coordination among religious congregations, as well as among other local or international agencies.

One of the recommendations stemming from the Conference, which in turn became the purpose of this project, related to the need to enhance the approach by religious personnel vis-à-vis trafficking by developing and testing a training module for religious personnel. This module would address the following topics: social prevention approaches to trafficking, victim assistance techniques, development of context appropriate awareness raising material and the creation of an anti-trafficking trans-national network.

The US Bureau for Population, Refugees and Migrants (PRM) funded the project, with IOM appointed as the leading agency in charge of researching the issue of collaboration among religious institutions.

The objectives were stated as follows:

- to develop, test and carry out training modules for religious personnel of various denominations dealing/to deal with social prevention of trafficking and assistance to victims;
- to draft guidelines and awareness raising material; and
- to create an anti-trafficking network among religious personnel.

The project activities as well as all the materials used during the project implementation were built in partnership with the following organizations[1]:

- UISG: International Union of Superiors General (female religious)
- USMI: Union of Major Superiors of Italy (female religious)
- ICMC/Fondazione Migrantes (Rome)

The first step envisaged the design of a training session tailored to the needs of sisters. For this task, both IOM and UISG/USMI appointed Stefano Volpicelli, Roberto Rossi, Sr. Bernadette Sangma, FMA and Sr. Eugenia Bonetti, MC as their respective professional trainers.

The training contents were organized sequentially, with seven steps (folders) presenting trafficking and counter-trafficking approaches.

The folders begin with an in-depth introduction to trafficking, which elucidate the "push-pull" factors, the victim profiles and health risks commonly associated with trafficking (folders 1-3).

Once the phenomenon is firmly grasped, then prevention activities intended for countries of origin and destination are considered.

An examination of the "helping relationship," as a proven support technique, follows.

Once the technique is introduced, understood, and practiced, then its intended result (empowerment of the victim) is explored at length.

Likewise, the limitations of the helping relationship, often perceived as failure by the "helper", are presented and discussed. This is a particularly important topic, since disregarding natural limitations can lead to frustration and eventual burnout.

Furthermore, in order to increase the programme's accessibility and relevance, regardless of whether one is working in policy and administrative levels or dealing directly with the victims, each folder is structured following the same format: from the general (explanations) to the specific (examples, strategies).

---

[1] Fondazione Migrantes left the project in 2005, USMI one year later.

This training conceptualisation can be summarised as follows:

General information	The intensity (simple knowledge of the phenomenon) → Major intensity (contact with the victims)						
	1	2	3	4	5	6	7
	The Framework	Victim's Profile	Health Risks	Prevention	Helping Relationship	Empower ment	Burn Out

Bearing in mind that the training course intends to meet the diverse expectations of religious sisters both from countries of origin and of destination, it has been designed to include as many issues as possible related to trafficking.

The training was always carried out by two leading trainers (one from IOM and one from UISG), supported by a local facilitator.

At the beginning, the project aimed at training sisters active in countries particularly affected by the phenomenon. The first two years were implemented having this objective in mind.

The strategy was modified in the third year. Following a joint assessment by UISG/IOM of the positive evaluation of the training (and a related follow-up session), it was decided to maximize the impact of the training, involving more representatives from different countries belonging to a particular geographical area.

From 2006 to 2010 this strategy was pursued, and it definitively boosted the involvement of religious sisters in counter-trafficking actions.

Another key point surfaced during 2008. Once again, UISG and IOM assessed the results of the previous years. The number of sisters trained was consistent, and the two agencies decided to organize a meeting in order to discuss strategies and compare the operational activities carried out. It was during that congress that the idea of a worldwide network began to take shape.

The following year, 2009, another congress was organized, this time aimed at setting up a network. The outcome of that network was the foundation of Talitha Kum.

The project ended in 2010, when it was decided that Talitha Kum could and should walk with its own feet. IOM remained an external supporting partners, and UISG started collecting funds from various sources.

And then...Talitha Kum

The main outcome of the 2009 Congress was an official request to the UISG Executive Board to establish an office in Rome with the aim of coordinating the existing networks at international level.

"Talitha Kum", the inspirational name for our Networks came from the Gospel of Mark, chapter 5, when Jesus ordered the young girl, who was apparently dead, to rise up and continue on living.

During the same year, the UISG Executive Board approved the request, and in 2010 nominated Sr. Estrella Castalone, FMA as the first coordinator.

Sr. Castalone was a former member of Talitha Kum Philippines, and coordinated Talitha Kum from 2010 to 2014. She established the basis of Talitha Kum as a network of sisters-led-networks, who operate on-the-ground, are grassroots-oriented and very committed to confront trafficking in persons.

Sr. Castalone oriented the activities of Talitha Kum, giving continuity to the training programs, especially in Latin America, South East Asia and Africa. She also initiated the official dialogue between Vatican Organizations and Talitha Kum in relation to human trafficking.

In May 2011, Talitha Kum / USIG called representatives from all the networks to Rome for the First International Coordination Committee of Talitha Kum. The aim of their gathering was to define the priorities for the Talitha Kum office in Rome. These were identified as: Formation, Networking and Communication.

In that same period, other networks joined Talitha Kum, and after five years Talitha Kum had a growing number of strong decentralised networks. However, the international connection was felt to be weak. This was the main challenge faced by Sr. Gabriella Bottani, SMC, the second coordinator of Talitha Kum, when she took over its coordination in January 2015. Until then, Sr. Bottani had been an active member of the "Um Grito pela Vida", the Brazilian network of Talitha Kum.

In February 2016, the Second International Coordination Committee of Talitha Kum was organized in Rome. The main priorities for the global network were confirmed as: Formation, Networking, Communication, while others were added: give visibility to human trafficking also through the work of the Sisters; more human and economic resources needed to support the anti-trafficking commitment; and to strengthen the collaboration against trafficking in persons in Sub-Saharan Africa and in the Middle East.

Since then Talitha Kum has developed several pilot projects to implement these priorities. The creation of the data base and the data collection is one the most important achievements.

The work started in 2017, but it took until 2018 before Talitha Kum saw the first concrete outcomes. The project is the result of the collaboration among Prof. Peter Lah, of the Department of Social Sciences at the Pontifical Gregorian University, Mr. Domenico Cosentino (the Engineer 4 Sigma snc), and all Talitha Kum leaders around the world.

Completing this journey has taken time and energy, particularly in order to collect and share information about the respective organization and activities within the Talitha Kum networks.

Concluding remarks

The first ten years of Talitha Kum are much more than the above chronology and order of events, facts and works over time. Our mission is ongoing, the weaving of encounters among religious sisters and brothers, along with many committed persons against human trafficking. In a very unique way, Talitha Kum encompasses the life histories of millions and millions of trafficked victims and survivors. They are the ones who reach out to us their hand, just as Jesus did with the young girl, inviting us to rise up, with courage and hope, so as to continue on together in our commitment against human trafficking.

Talitha Kum – International Network
of Consecrated Life Against Trafficking in Persons

Talitha Kum[2] is an international network of Consecrated Life against trafficking in persons founded in 2009. Working as a network facilitates collaboration and the interchange of information between consecrated men and women in 76 countries. The network is sponsored by the International Union of Superiors General (UISG), in collaboration with the Union of Superiors General (USG).

It arose from the shared desire to coordinate and strengthen the already-existing activities against trafficking undertaken by consecrated persons in the five continents. Talitha Kum is a network of networks, organized in many different ways, each promoting initiatives against trafficking in persons in their particular contexts and cultures.

Since its foundation, Talitha Kum continues to promote courses for the training of new local networks and to encourage networking and collaboration with other organizations working against trafficking in persons.

The goals of Talitha Kum are:
- To promote networking between consecrated persons, social organizations, religious and political leaders at national and international level;
- To strengthen the existing activities and initiatives, optimizing the resources of the consecrated life, to promote preventative actions, awareness raising, protection and assistance of victims as well as official reporting of trafficking;
- To develop educational programs for raising the awareness of this phenomenon, (and to enhance the professional responses of our members); and
- To act prophetically - condemning the exploitation of persons for economic or other motives and promoting campaigns aimed at changing of attitudes and practices.

---

[2] Source: http://www.talithakum.info/ Accessed March 1, 2018.

Part I: Census 2015

Peter Lah, S.J. | Diego Meza | Doramiène Djarba

In 2015 the coordinator of the global network commissioned the first systematic collection of data about national and regional networks. This report is based on the questionnaire obtained in response to this initiative. A total of 34 valid questionnaires were returned. Seven were discarded because the respondents were in fact associated with more than one budding networks.

1.1. General overview

Table 1.1 lists the countries that were represented in the 2015 census. N.B.: the majority of respondents were national networks of women religious against trafficking in human persons. There were however also regional networks and those that involve more than one country.

Africa	Cameroon Nigeria South Africa Zambia	4
Latin America	Nicaragua Peru El Salvador Guatemala Honduras Argentina Uruguay Costa Rica Brasil	9
U.S.A. and Canada	U.S.A.	1
Australia and Oceania	Australia New Zeland	2

Asia	Philippines Thailand Indonesia East Timor Korea Hong Kong Taiwan	7
Europe	Albania Netherlands Germany Poland Renate (regional network in Europe)	4

Table 1.1: Talitha Kum members who responded to the 2015 questionnaire, by country and continent.

Table 1.1 reveals two peculiarities. First, there are few responses from Africa. We have only four networks that have responded to the questionnaire. One can only speculate about the reasons for this void. Possible explanations include a scarce availability of the internet (the questionnaire was sent out via email) and a generally weaker culture of administrative reporting practices. Second, Europe presents itself as a very differentiated reality. Some networks are limited to the nation in which they are based, whereas others are multi-national, even Europe-wide. There is certain overlap between national and multinational networks. For this reason it is difficult to provide the exact number of countries in which Talitha Kum is present.

1.2. Characteristics of networks

In their most basic forms, networks are often no more than **committees and coordinating groups** that meet regularly. At this stage, they do not have own structures. Instead, they are hosted and supported by participating congregations. For example, the ANZRATH (New Zealand) reported bi-monthly meetings in the capital. Talitha Kum Thailand met every six months in order to prepare a report for the Conference of Major superiors, drawing upon resources, namely office space, provided by different Congregations. Bakhita is a section operating under the Council of Major Superiors in Poland. Red

Kawsay (Uruguay) is a committee of the Conference of the Religious responsible for annual planning and evaluation of activities in the area of human trafficking. Similarly, Talitha Kum Korea operates within the nation's Conference of Women Religious. Their aim is primarily that of networking (information, sharing of experiences) various activities of member in the area of human trafficking.

On the opposite end of the spectrum we find **fully fledged organizations with clear structure and resources**. Examples of it are: ACRATH in Australia (which has an ecclesial judicial status and is also incorporated in civil law), in addition to officers of the Association and its governing bodies has a national executive officer who collaborates closely with regional coordinators and local groups; SRTV, in the Netherlands; the Medaille Trust (U.K.) has its own board of trustees that appoints a project director who in turn manages four service managers who deliver services from seven houses. SOLWODI (Germany) runs 17 counselling centers and 6 women's shelters.

The Renate is perhaps the most mature network of women religious in the area of anti-trafficking. It is an old network operating in twenty European states and has built considerable knowledge and experience. It employs three people: a secretary and website manager, a communications officer, and a finance officer. Its structure consists of the Core Group, the Steering committee, and four working groups: education resources, survivor support, legislative advocacy and communications). Among their operation methods they list: regular communication and coordination among the members, regular exchange of information among members, annual strategic planning meeting of the core group, annual training for specific subject related to anti-trafficking, sharing of materials, toolkits, ideas for prayer via a webpage, meeting key people involved in anti-trafficking who represent the Catholic Church and other relevant actors with the goal of shaping public opinion, awareness raising at all levels, providing financial support to members of the network, mapping and analysis of anti-trafficking initiatives.

In between these models we find networks with elements of structural autonomy and resources. This is particularly true of larger scale networks and those that comprise several states. The Um Grito pela Vida (an activity of the consecrated life in Brazil) comprises 23 groups across the nation and is coordinated by a staff of three in the national office as well as one for each region. Kawsay Argentina and Kawsay Uruguay each have an executive secretary, as well as one person whose task is to interface with local providers and national conferences of religious. Talitha Kum Philippines serves as the secretariat for participating countries of Southeast Asia. In addition to their role in consolidating countries' initiatives for publication and information they assist with supervision, monitoring and networking.

Finally, we find the networks in Africa, which develop their activities in association with other organizations such as NGOs, religious communities and evangelical churches. These networks not only focus on human trafficking but develop other activities. For example, COSUDOW Network of Nigeria works against sexual exploitation, child abuse, child labor, and abuses against the dignity of women.

1.3. Activities of networks

In this section only those activities are presented that support the networks' principal mission. The activities of networks aimed "ad intra » – meaning that they serve principally to sustain and grow the network – will be presented in the section "Functions ad intra ».

To boost the effectiveness in working against trafficking in persons, on 15 November 2000, the United Nations adopted a protocol to prevent, suppress and punish trafficking in persons, especially women and children. It supplements the United Nations Convention against Transnational Organized Crime. This agreement, known as the *Palermo Protocol*[3], establishes four levels of action:

---

[3] Adopted by General Assembly resolution 55/25, is supplementing the UN Convention. It entered into force on 25 December 2003. The Protocol to Prevent, Suppress and Punish Trafficking in Persons, especially Women and Children is the first global legally binding instrument with an agreed definition on trafficking in persons. The Protocol contains provisions on a range of issues, including criminalisation, assistance to and protection for victims, the status of victims in the receiving states, repatriation of victims, preventive measures, actions to discourage the demand, exchange of information and training, and measures to strengthen the effectiveness of border controls. The protocol stipulates that states parties must adopt or strengthen legislative or other measures to discourage the demand that fosters all forms of exploitation of persons, especially women and children that leads to trafficking. States must become parties to the Convention before they can become parties to any of its Protocol.

1. To prevent and combat trafficking in persons, paying particular attention to women and children (**Prevention**).
2. To protect and assist the victims of such trafficking, with full respect for their human rights (**Protection**).
3. To promote cooperation among States Parties in order to meet those objectives (**Prosecution**).
4. The strengthening of partnerships and coordination (**Partnership**).

All Talihta Kum's networks carry out activities in each of these categories. We can identify:

1. Development of educational and information resources that are shared through various media (commonly, social networks). These instruments are used in the context of formation in religious congregations, at meetings of bishops and priests, in Catholic schools and universities, with groups of young people and families. The objectives of this formation initiatives include: raising awareness, analyzing causes and impact, determining risks and vulnerable areas, reflecting on how faith affects one's response, and determining what actions can be taken.
2. At the second level, the networks are active in prosecution and in action to influence policy and legislation (lobbying). They also conduct activities of reporting abuses, rescue of victims, rehabilitation and care of the victims, and the provision of shelters. Last but not least, members provide integration courses, helplines, social work in the streets, repatriation projects and provide financial loans. The spiritual dimension has been important. Some networks have organized prayer days and the service of the spiritual direction for the victims. These activities (i.e., second level), aimed directly at combatting the phenomenon and its effects account for the bulk of networks' work.
3. The third level concerns the relations between the states. It involves bilateral or multilateral collaboration aimed at mitigating factors that contribute to persons' being more vulner-

able for trafficking, such as poverty, underdevelopment and the lack of equitable opportunities particularly for the youth and women. The same work should be developed in the areas of education and legislation, without forgetting the operability that is translated in information exchange, control of the borders, review of documents, etc. Although the activities are varied, Talitha Kum networks act discreetly at this level.

4. At the fourth level, the initiatives on strengthening partnerships and coordination occur through its participation with other agencies. For example, Australian Catholic Religious Against Trafficking in Humans (ACRATH) works together with Anti-Slavery Australia and Salvation Army Safe House. Cooperation includes working together with non-governmental organizations, other relevant organizations and other sectors of civil society. For example, in Costa Rica the religious are active in several areas: awareness raising, education, and advocacy – jointly with the governmental and non-governmental institutions – in favor of populations at risk. They have specific initiatives aimed at preventing the phenomenon and helping the victims. Trafficking survivors, NGOs, faith groups, donors, academics, and businesses have skills and perspectives that, when combined, will drive innovation and bring sustained progress to the fight against human trafficking. Governments have a vital role in bringing together stakeholders and creating partnerships.

The four levels of action are presented and discussed in greater detail in subsequent sections.

1. Prevention and combat against trafficking in persons: Commonly employed methods

Most of the networks carry out work at this level, probably because the conditions and facilities in each country allow it. Other reasons could be: the cost, the availability of human resources and the young age of these structures. Tables 1.2 and 1.3 provide a summary view of methods employed.

	Country	Awareness campaigns & formation	Social media campaigns	Research projects
Africa	Cameroon	X		
	Nigeria	X	X	
	South Africa	X		
	Zambia	X		
Latin America	Argentina	X	X	
	Brazil	X	X	
	Costa Rica	X		
	El Salvador	X	X	
	Guatemala	X	X	X
	Honduras	X		
	Nicaragua	X	X	
	Peru	X		
	Uruguay	X	X	
U.S.A. & Canada	U.S.A.	X	X	X
Asia	East Timor			
	Hong Kong			
	Indonesia			
	Korea			
	Philippines	X		X
	Taiwan			
	Thailand			
Australia and Oceania	Australia	X	X	
	New Zealand	X	X	
Europe	Albania	X	X	
	Croatia	X		
	Czech Reoublic	X	X	
	Hungary			
	Germany	X		
	Malta	X	X	
	Netherlands	X		
	Poland	X	X	
	Slovakia			
	UK	X		
Total	33	25	14	3

Table 1.2: Overview of main activities by countries: Prevention and combat against trafficking in persons

	Awareness campaigns	Publicity & activism on social media	Educational activities w/groups	Research projects
Asia	x		x	x
Central America	x		x	
Europe	x			x
Uruguay, Peru, Argentina	x	x	x	x
Total	4	1	3	3

Table 1.3: List of main activities by regional networks: Prevention and combat against trafficking in persons

Awareness campaigns: Most networks are trying to raise awareness about this crime. This objective is achieved through the campaigns in schools, churches, religious organizations and the media. This activity involves the dissemination of information about the seriousness of human trafficking. For instance, Croatia's Network promotes awareness through conferences for priests at clergy meetings, at parish Masses, in religious communities, and students groups – especially those who are interested in human rights and the social teaching of the Church.

Publicity and activism through media/ means of social communication: These networks have prepared some materials to be spread through different media and communities. Among the media more used are: radio, television, newspapers (at national, local and diocesan level, as well as in parish newsletters) and the internet. Many respondents indicated their use of social networks through which they share information about their activities. They organize activities with journalists or train specialized personnel to carry out this type of activities. The Honduras Network has organized training sessions for journalists and social communicators in the country while the US Network has a communications working group which is responsible for USCSAHT's media presence and oversees the maintenance and updating of its website, its Facebook page and its Twitter account. Other networks produced resources about human trafficking. Among these materials are: leaflets for prison governors and chaplains and a speaker's pack that includes information, resources, and prayer material.

Educational activities with different groups: The networks organize meetings with different participants: students, priests, religious, members of the government, teachers and parents. These projects involve training people in the main elements related to human trafficking. Experts on the subject participate in these meetings. They may be members of the network or work in others institutions. For example, the Guatemala Network has organized workshops with religious communities, schools, institutes and universities with students and teachers, catechists, youth groups and parish groups. Especially, they have held 12 pedagogical days for teachers from the municipality of Tecún Umán, San Marcos, at the border between Guatemala and Mexico. In Africa, there are two innovative projects specifically tailored to local situations. The networks of South Africa and Zambia have a training project for truckers against human trafficking. The Nigerian network offers a training project for young people and families and gives scholarships to indigent students.

Research projects: This activity includes research on the phenomena of human trafficking. It is closely related to on-going formation of members as well as of the general public. These studies try to identify their causes, dynamics and actors. This work includes material for the training of the agents involved in this task, as well as for the dissemination in the media. In 2014, the Guatemala network developed an investigation on the survivors of trafficking across the Guatemala-Mexico border. Moreover, the Philippines network developed and produced a training module based on faith and gender.

2. Protection of and assistance to victims

A significant number of networks are involved in the protection and assistance to victims. First of all, we must note that one of the strongest fronts in the fight against human trafficking is the reporting of this crime and social intervention. This requires more experience and expertise in this field. Poland, Brazil, Czech Republic are recognized for their initiatives and activism in the street. Tables 1.4 and 1.5 provide a summary view of commonly-employed methods.

	Country	Lobbying & advocacy	Material support	National help lines	Spiritual & psychological support	Judicial support
Africa	Cameroon	x				x
	Nigeria		x		x	
	South Africa	x	x		x	x
	Zambia	x	x		x	x
Latin America	Argentina					
	Brazil		x			x
	Costa Rica					
	El Salvador				x	x
	Guatemala		x			
	Honduras					
	Nicaragua					x
	Peru	x	x			
	Uruguay					
U.S.A. & Canada	U.S.A.	x	x			
Asia	East Timor					
	Hong Kong					
	Indonesia					
	Korea					
	Philippines					x
	Taiwan					
	Thailand					
Australia and Oceania	Australia	x	x			x
	New Zeland	x				
Europe	Alabania		x			
	Croatia					
	The Czech Republic	x	x			
	Hungary					
	Germany		x			
	Malta		x			
	The Netherlands	x				

Poland		x	x	x	
Slovakia					
UK	x	x			
Total	**33**	**10**	**14**	**1**	**5**	**8**

Table 1.4: Protection of, and assistance to the victims. Main activities by countries

	Lobbying and advocay	Collaborative actions w/ institutions	Assistance & protection	Economic & material support	National help lines	Spiritual support	Complaints & pleadings
Asia	x	x					
Central America							
Europe	x		x				
Uruguay, Peru & Argentina		x	x				x
Total	**2**	**2**	**2**	**0**	**0**	**0**	**1**

Table 1.5: Protection of, and assistance to the victims. Main activities by regional networks

Lobbying and Advocacy: These activities include actions to influence policy and legislation, submission to government inquiries, visits to, and interviews with, elected officials with the scope of supporting the legislation that address human trafficking issues. Australia Network advocates with Members of Parliament whose ministerial portfolios include the issue of human trafficking, e.g., ministers for Justice, Immigration & Border Protection, Foreign Affairs, Social Services. Talitha Kum Southeast Asia tries to empower, organize and mobilize the women religious to influence legislation, regulation, or other government decisions, actions, or policies in order to respond to and counter human trafficking.

Assistance and Protection: The networks provide support to survivors and intensive training on the rescue, rehabilitation, aftercare and reintegration of victims. This level includes social work in night clubs, at national frontiers and in high-risk places; social counselling; assistance provided in dealing with police and legal matters; psychological support; assistance with the legalization of their status in the country; support to victims who became witnesses against traffickers; and integration measures, such as language courses, vocational training, drama, art and culture projects. For example, a sister of Holy Cross in Czech Republic works as a street worker in night clubs and with women in street prostitution. In Poland, the Bakhita Network has a program of protection and support for victims and witnesses of human trafficking. People can collaborate with the police and break with perpetrators.

Economic and material support: Networks provide transport for the victims within the country; they offer extended help with the safe return to the country of origin, a shelter for a safe accommodation, provision of beds, clothes, medications and financial help in the process of reintegration. SOLWODI in Germany provides micro-credits to the victims, and Bakhita in Poland helps the person in recovering her place in society and rebuilding her life. This assistance includes provisions of items necessary for everyday life as well as educational support (acquiring a degree, learning a profession, and assistance in entering the job market).

National Help Lines: It is a special service for emergencies and complaints, as well as for psychological help. Bakhita in Poland has a 24/7 helpline for victims and witnesses of human trafficking.

Spiritual Support: This service includes days of prayer for the victims and also spiritual counselling for them. For instance, Ramá Network in Nicaragua has organized a prayer day with the participation of different organizations. The Nigerian network offers a spiritual direction service called "Welcoming home" where the victims are helped to recover through counselling and spiritual direction.

Reporting and Pleadings: Some networks report sexual exploitation and trafficking of people to the media and the authorities. In addition, they follow up on specific cases. Ramá in Guatemala has reported to authorities six cases of sexual exploitation of a minor.

3. Promotion and Cooperation among States Parties to the Convention

Australia, Germany, Netherlands and Europe Network have been involved with international organizations who support the victims. It is understandable that Talitha Kum networks are not more actively engaged in initiatives under this heading since it refers to the states who are parties to the Palermo Protocol. Even though the networks are not states, they nevertheless can effectively work across national borders as they cooperate with other members of the network.

4. The strengthening of partnerships and coordination

Most networks work in cooperation with other organizations: religious, governmental or non-governmental. The list includes: Caritas, the national conferences of religious communities, episcopal conferences, the police, judges, universities, and organizations defending human rights. For example, a Talitha Kum person in Slovakia participates in the expert group advising the Ministry of the Interior; URAT in Albania works with the Peace Corps; Talita Kum in Korea is working for North Korean Defectors; ACRATH in Australia support the victims in collaboration with Anti-Slavery Australia and Salvation Army Safe House; and CTIP in South Africa works with other religious institutions, such as the Salvation Army, Evangelical Lutheran Women of the East Rand, and Interfaith Counter Trafficking.

	Country	Joint actions with other institutions
Africa	Cameroon	
	Nigeria	x
	South Africa	x
	Zambia	x
Latin America	Argentina	
	Brazil	x
	Costa Rica	
	El Salvador	x
	Guatemala	x
	Honduras	
	Nicaragua	
	Peru	
	Uruguay	x
U.S. and Canada	U.S.A.	
Asia	East Timor	
	Hong Kong	
	Indonesia	
	Korea	x
	Philippines	x
	Taiwan	
	Thailand	
Australia & Oceania	Australia	
	New Zealand	
Europe	Albania	x
	Croatia	
	Czech Republic	x
	Hungary	
	Germany	x
	Malta	x
	The Netherlands	
	Poland	x
	Slovakia	x
	UK	

Table 1.6:
List of networks
reporting joint actions
with other institutions,
by country.

Networks	Joint actions with other institutions
Asia	x
Central America	
Europe	
Uruguay, Peru & Argentina	x

Table 1.7: List of regional networks reporting
joint actions with other institutions.

1.4. Functions ad intra

While the overwhelming share of reported activities is directed outward, that is towards the (potential) victims, important stakeholders in policy-making, prevention, and prosecution, as well as toward the general population, there are certain activities that primarily benefit the organization or network itself. Those activities include:

- Building alliances and partnerships with similar organizations
- Exchanging relevant information
- Formation, for example in language and specific skills
- Mutual support, both formal and informal

Strengthening of partnership (not limited to organizations that are engaged in combatting the trafficking) represents an activity where a regional network can be very important. Talitha Kum Southeast Asia speaks about "networking with the major religious superiors throughout the region with the aim of making the issue of trafficking in humans a priority." Through partnerships they empower, organize and mobilize the women religious in the Southeast Asia region to respond to and counter human trafficking, especially of women and children. Partnerships make it more effective to influence policy and legislation through lobbying.

Bakhita highlights the importance of information collection and sharing in combatting the phenomenon and helping victims: "Workshops and seminaries (for members of the network) allow for the development of efficient and professional assistance to victims." Similarly, Renate offers to its members information and education resources, e.g., training, English language course.

Relationship between the network and the conference of religious

As mentioned in the presentation of Talitha Kum structure, individual networks are staffed by women religious from various congregations. Thus they do not fall under the oversight of traditional orders and congregations. Rather, they report to respective (national) conferences or major religious superiors. Respondents overwhelmingly emphasized a very good relationship of cooperation and support.

What can the network (regional, national, global Talitha Kum) do to make your work more effective?

Nineteen networks, of which three were regional networks, responded to this question. The responses were classified in four categories.

	Country	Information, dialogue, sharing, networking & collaboration	Formation, awareness building, coordination, prosecution	Reciprocal support, incl. resources	Representation to religious, social & political authorities
Africa	Cameroon		x		
Asia	Philippines	x	x		
	Thailand	x	x	x	
	Regional South Asia	x	x	x	
America	Argentina	x	x	x	x
	Brazil	x	x		x
	El Salvador	x	x		x
	Honduras	x			x
	Nicaragua	x	x	x	
	Peru	x	x		
	Uruguay	x	x	x	
	USA	x	x	x	
	Regional Kawsay	x	x		
	Regional Rama	x	x	x	x

	Malta	x	x		x
	Netherlands	x			
Europe	Poland	x	x		
	UK	x	x	x	
	Renate	x	x	x	

Table 1.8: What can Talitha Kum do to make national
and regional networks' activities more effective?

The respondents in the **first category** emphasized their interest in receiving up-to-date information from Rome concerning human trafficking and anything else that relates to it, such as social, political and legal aspects of the phenomenon. This will make their work more effective. For example, the regional network in Europe suggested that the Rome office inform the members about new initiatives and trends in the field; present important member networks and effective methods of work; and organize periodical campaigns in which all networks could take part. It suggested that the main web page be made accessible in various languages. A meeting of all member networks every 3-5 years would allow members worldwide to get to know each other and would thus make their communication easier. The U.S. network looks favorably at the opportunity to connect with an international group of women religious because it offers the opportunity to share and learn from the experiences of others, to share information, resources and good practices.

The **second group** of answers deals with aspects of formation, awareness raising, and prosecution. For example, Cameroon reported their interest in learning from the experience of Talitha Kum. In particular, they are interested in how to work in a network. According to respondents, the global network must provide formation to its members with the goal of improving the effectiveness and efficiency of their work. All networks should act as prophetic voices of denunciation as well as a proactive force for change within the Church and vis-à-vis international institutions. There are various ways to sensitize people about human trafficking. For example, the

U.S. emphasizes the need for formation on specific problems, such as gender equality and exploitation of labor. Here, the Philippines network emphasized the importance of building a cross-referenced database of victims.

The **third topic** that emerged relates to financial autonomy of networks. The U.S. network, for example, mentioned the importance of organizing a forum dedicated to discussing the development of a strategic plan for Talitha Kum's activities, particularly in view of their financial sustainability. Almost all respondents mentioned the issue of financial and material support, particularly as they relate to common activities and to production and diffusion of informational resources, as well as in the area of prevention.

Fourth, certain respondents mentioned the role of the central office in representing their activities to religious, social and political actors, thus rendering their efforts more effective. They affirm the importance of networks to spearhead the efforts by the Church towards an effective change in the fight against human trafficking. The crucial role of the central office in facilitating exchange, sharing, and prayer was also mentioned by several networks. Finally, the U.S. network asked for the outcome of the census to be shared with all members of the network. Not only is it useful to have this information, it undoubtedly would boost the morale of those who at the grass roots level are involved in this difficult fight.

Part II: Census 2018

Peter Lah S.J. | Diego Meza | Mayra Daniela Cuellar Rojas

2.1. Introduction

Building upon the 2015 census and survey of Talitha Kum networks, a systematic, streamlined survey was designed with the intent to, first, gather the basic information of the rapidly growing and maturing reality and, second, to assess its effectiveness. The new questionnaire consisted of 22 open questions organized into two sections: the first was dedicated to the structure of networks, and the second to objectives and activities. Representatives of individual networks were asked about their various activities as they relate to Talitha Kum core mission. In mapping the activities of the networks, we followed the classification of the Protocol of Palermo which defines the four basic areas of action, namely: Prevention, Protection, Prosecution and Partnership.

At the end of the questionnaire representatives were asked to indicate activities that were most rewarding or most challenging, and to indicate what could be done to improve the effectiveness of their work.

Building upon our previous experience with data collection, we followed the following procedure. An on-line database was constructed and each representative was given a possibility to respond to the questionnaire in a way that directly fed their answers into the database. Given the enormous disparities with regard to respondents' access to IT infrastructure and their level of information literacy, alternative methods for answering the questionnaire were provided, such as mailing the answers to a contact person in Rome. The contact person and two research assistants organized the data and, where necessary, followed up with requests for clarifications and additional information. In the final step, the errors were corrected and a "clean" database was produced for final analysis of responses.

The analysis and presentation of qualitative data is rather straightforward. We sought to be as non-directive with our questions as possible. On the other hand, we strove towards a certain uniformity and systematicity. The analysis of activities in individual areas of the Palermo Protocol consisted in grouping them under more general categories. The latter basically emerged from the data we obtained from respondents: they were not developed deductively as a result of a prior theoretical work.

In addition to gathering information about networks' activities, we also asked for a quantifiable assessment of their reach, or of the impact of their activities. We believe the figures concerning the number of volunteer collaborators to be reasonably reliable. Taking into consideration that activities which in this report are presented distinctly (prevention, protection, etc.) may in reality overlap to a significant degree, we advise against adding up the numbers across the areas. For example: a volunteer who works in the area of prevention may well be engaged in the area of protection as well, with the result of being counted twice.

In the case of the number of people that were helped or reached, the reported figures must be interpreted as conservative estimates of true reach. While it is easy to keep track of web site or social engagement, it is already more difficult to estimate the number of pupils or parishioners participating in Talitha Kum sponsored activities, and it is next to impossible to determine the size of media audiences. We invite the reader to take the reported figures as a conservative estimate of the true reach of named activities.

In all, 44 networks responded to our questionnaire by January 31st, 2019. Two were excluded because they are in fact regional networks, in contrast to the majority that are national in scope. The resulting statistics are represented in Table 2.1.

	Number of networks contacted	Number of responses
Africa	10	8
Asia	12	12
Europe	8	5
Oceania	2	2
Latin America	14	13
U.S. and Canada	2	2
TOTAL	**48**	**42**

Table 2.1: Talitha Kum networks.

In subsequent sections we will present and discuss the responses to seven questions. The first four concern the four areas of activity in the fight against human trafficking. The final three are dedicated to networks' self-assessment of their work.

2.2. General overview

There are four types of networks: national, regional, continental and global. In total there are 47 national networks, 10 regional networks, 5 continental networks and one global network, namely the Talitha Kum office in Rome. In total, the census comprised 62 networks, not counting the global office in Rome.

For comparison: 36 groups responded to the questionnaire that was the foundation for the census of 2015. In the intervening years, the network grew, the characteristics of certain members became more clearly defined, and - last but not least - we were successful at improving the response rate.

2.2.1. National Networks

The data base contains 42 national networks, of whom 34 have completed the questionnaire, two have returned incomplete questionnaires and the other 6 have not answered. Table 1 lists the national networks that were represented in the 2018 census and indicates the status of their responses.

Continent	Country	Complete	Incomplete	No response
Africa	Talitha Kum – Nigeria	x		
	Talitha Kum – Cameroon	x		
	CTIP – Zimbabwe	x		x
	Talitha Kum – Burkina Faso	x		
	RATH – Kenya	x		
	CTIP – South Africa			
Total	6	5		1
Asia	CWTC-IBSI – Indonesia	x		
	Talitha Kum – Myanmar	x		
	Talitha Kum – Pakistan	x		x
	Talitha Kum – Cambodia		x	
	AMRAT – Sri Lanka	x		
	Talitha Kum – Thailand	x		
	Talitha Kum – Philippines	x		
	Talitha Kum – East Timor	x		
	AMRAT – Talitha Kum India	x		
	Talitha Kum – South Korea	x		
	Talitha Kum – Japan			
Total	11	9	1	1
America	Red Tamar – Colombia	x		
	USCSAHT – U.S.A.	x		
	CATHII – Canada	x	x	
	Red Ramà – Guatemala			x
	Red Ramà – Panama	x		
	Red Ramà – Nicaragua	x		
	Um Grito pela Vida – Brasil	x		
	Santo Domingo	x		
	Red Rahamim – Mexico	x		
	Red Kawsay – Peru	x		
	Red Ramà – Honduras	x		
	Red Kawsay – Paraguay	x		
	Red Kawsay – Argentina	x		
	Red Jaire – Costa Rica			
	Red Kawsay – Uruguay			
	Red Ramà – El Salvador			
Total	16	14	1	1

Europe	APT – Ireland				x
	USMI RETE – Italy		x		
	BAKHITA – Poland				x
	SOLWODI – Deutschland		x		x
	PRO Demnitatea femeii – Romania		x		
	CAVITP – Portugal		x		
	URAT – Albania				
Total		7	4		3
Oceania	ANZRATH – New Zealand		x		
	ACRATH – Australia		x		
Total		2	2		
TOTAL		42	34	2	6

Table 2.2: National networks

Table 2.2 reveals that in Africa there are six national networks, of which five have completed the questionnaire. In Asia, there are 11 national networks, of whom 9 have completed the questionnaire, one provided an incomplete questionnaire and one failed to respond. In America there are 16 national networks, of whom 14 have completed the questionnaire, one has an incomplete questionnaire and one has not answered. In Europe there are seven national networks, of whom four have completed the questionnaire and three have not answered. In Oceania, there are two national networks, both of whom have completed the questionnaire.

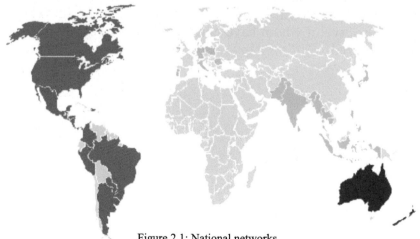

Figure 2.1: National networks.

2.2.2. Regional Networks

Table 2.3 lists the regional networks that were represented in the 2018 census. This table includes the status of their questionnaires.

Continent	Network	Complete	Incomplete
Africa	Counter trafficking in persons (CTIP)	x	
Total	1	1	
Asia	(AMRAT) Regional Asia Talitha Kum South East Asia	x	x
Total	2	1	1
America	Red Kawsay Red Ramà	x x	
Total	2	2	
Europe	Renate	x	
Total	1	1	
TOTAL	6	5	1

Table 2.3: Regional networks

Africa and in Europe each have one regional network. Both provided a complete response. In Asia there are two regional networks, of whom one of them has completed the questionnaire. In America there are two regional networks that have completed the questionnaire. In summary, there are a total of six regional networks, five of whom have completed the survey, and one has not answered.

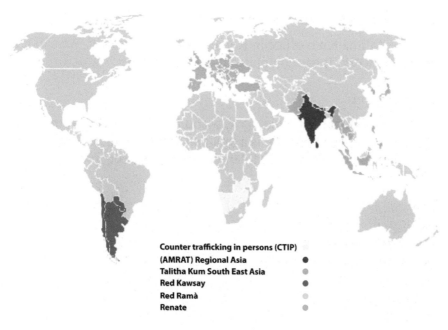

Figure 2.2: Regional networks

2.2.3. Continental Networks

Table 2.4 lists the continental networks that were represented in the 2018 census. This table include the status of their questionnaires.

Network	Complete	Incomplete	No response
Talitha Kum Africa			x
Talitha Kum ASIA	x		
Comision Trata CLAR	x		
Talitha Kum Oceania		x	
TOTAL (4)	2	1	1

Table 2.4: Continental networks

Table 2.4 reveals that there are one network for each continent. Two of them have completed the questionnaire, two of them have not responded, and one has provided an incomplete questionnaire.

2.2.4. Worldwide Network

The Talitha Kum office in Rome has a special status. We call it a global network. It has completed the questionnaire.

2.2.5 Sections

Some national networks have sections. They are listed in Table 2.5. A subdivision typically is a unit that reports to the main (national) office and works in a well-defined area of the country.

Network	Country	Number of sections
Um Grito pela Vida Brasil	Brasil	30
AMRAT - Talitha Kum India	India	19
Talitha Kum South Korea	Korea	11
Red Kawsay Argentina	Argentina	11
Red Kawsay Peru	Peru	8
Red Rahamim Mexico	Mexico	6
ACRATH (Australian Catholic Religious Against Trafficking in Humans)	Australia	5
Red Tamar Colombia	Colombia	5
CWTC-IBSI - Indonesia	Indonesia	5
USMI RETE "ANTI-TRATTA"	Italy	4
Talitha kum Thailand	Thailand	4
Aotearoa New Zealand religious against trafficking in humans - (ANZRATH)	New Zealand	3
Red Ramà Nicaragua	Nicaragua	3
Talitha Kum Pakistan	Pakistan	3
Talitha Kum Philippines	Philippines	3
Talitha Kum Cameroon	Cameroon	2
Talitha Kum - Nigeria	Nigeria	2
TOTAL	17	124

Table 2.5: Networks with sections

Seventeen networks reported at least two active sections. It should not surprise that more populous countries (e.g. India) and/or those that cover more territory, e.g., Brazil, should adopt this type of organization.

2. 3. Characteristics of networks: Staff

From the 2015 census a picture of great variety among networks' structure emerged. This can be explained by the fact that various initiatives were in their early stages of development and furthermore had to find ways to operate in many different social and political contexts. Some of them had been in existence long before Talitha Kum was founded as a global initiative, others were just beginning to operate.

In the intervening years the networks matured. Furthermore, informed by the experience of the 2015 survey, we decided to focus our attention to the "primary unit" of Talitha Kum, as it were, namely to national networks. This made the comparison easier and more meaningful. Other types were excluded from this analysis.

Respondents were asked to indicate the number of full-time collaborators (staff) and also to provide an approximate number of part-time collaborators. One case (Solwodi) was excluded from this analysis because it was very unlike others. For example, it has a full-time staff of 200 persons, double the number of all other networks combined.

When the remaining networks are analyzed, we find 103 persons working full time, i.e., more than half of their time, in the context of Talitha Kum. In addition to those, 1,719 part-time collaborators were indicated.

A closer look at the statistics reveals that only 16 networks (23%) reported having at least one full-time staff person. Three quarters of Talitha Kum networks make do without full-time personnel. It would appear that the number of full-time employees is strongly correlated to the gross domestic product of the country in which the network is headquartered. It is less strongly correlated to the size of the country or to the complexity of a network.

The situation changes dramatically when we look at part-time collaborators. The networks having 3 or more sections (15 networks,

20%) reported having 1381 part-time collaborators (80% of the to-tal). In contrast to full-time personnel, of which 77% of networks had none, almost half of networks reported having at least one part-time collaborator.

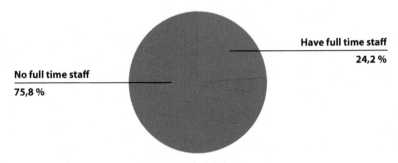

Figure 2.3: Full-time staff (N=67)

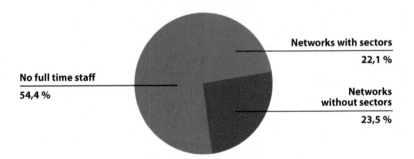

Figure 2.4: Part-time staff (N=67)

Part III: Areas of activity

Peter Lah S.J. | Diego Meza | Mayra Daniela Cuellar Rojas

In our analyses of networks' activities we follow the classification proposed by the so called "Protocol of Palermo" (see above, Section 1.3).

3.1 Prevention

In Table 3.1, various activities aimed at the prevention of human trafficking are presented.

	Country	Awareness campaigns & formation	Social media campaigns	Supporting persons at risk	No answer
Africa	Burkina Faso	x			
	Cameroon				x
	Ghana	x			
	Kenya	x			
	Nigeria	x	x	x	
	South Africa	x			
	Tunisia	x	x		
	Uganda				x
	Zambia				x
	Zimbabwe	x	x		
Latin America	Argentina	x	x		
	Brazil	x	x		
	Colombia	x		x	
	Costa Rica	x			
	El Salvador	x	x		
	Guatemala	x	x		
	Honduras	x	x	x	
	Mexico	x			
	Nicaragua	x			

Region	Country					
	Panama					x
	Paraguay	x	x			
	Peru	x	x			
	Dominican Republic	x				
	Uruguay	x				
U.S.A. & Canada	Canada					x
	U.S.A.	x	x			
Asia	Cambodia					x
	East Timor	x				
	Japan	x	x			
	India		x	x		
	Indonesia	x				
	Korea	x	x			
	Myamar	x				
	Malaysia					x
	Pakistan					
	Philippines	x				
	Sri Lanka	x				
	Thailand	x				
Australia & Oceania	Australia		x			
	New Zealand	x				
Europe	Albania					x
	Germany	x	x			
	Ireland					x
	Italy	x	x	x		
	Poland					
	Romania	x				
	Portugal					x
Total		47	33	17	5	10

Table 3.1: activities in the area of prevention

Training and awareness campaigns: Most networks carry out continuous training of its members through workshops or seminars for a greater knowledge of the problem and for a context-appropriate action. They engage in the formation of leaders who are active in various areas such as: in the educational institutions, among members of religious communities, pastoral agents, community leaders, and members of the various associations working in the area of human trafficking. The scope is to initiate, disseminate and strengthen the awareness of the problem of trafficking in human persons. Furthermore, specific training for women, often those considered at risk, is provided as a form of prevention. All networks are engaged in promoting awareness about this crime. This objective is achieved through various campaigns, educational activities and workshops that are mainly offered in schools, parishes, religious organizations and through social media. Specifically, these activities include dissemination of information on the severity of trafficking, and the importance of recognizing the mechanisms at work, especially in environments considered to be at greater risk. In Thailand, for example, awareness campaigns against trafficking are offered to various groups at all levels: religious persons, priests, bishops, students, young people, adults, and tribal groups in the border area. Another important form of awareness and testimony are days of prayer against trafficking in persons, and the dissemination of the various celebrations highlighting the problems of women, child labor and migrants.

Media campaigns: Another important form of prevention is the dissemination of information about the problem of trafficking in persons through different media. Commonly-used means of communication are: radio, television, newspapers (at national, local and diocesan level, as well as in parish newsletters) and the Internet. The aim of these campaigns is to share information on their activities and to publicize prayer days against trafficking. Peru, for example, has created and circulated a documentary for raising awareness and prevention, and the United States carries out training activities through their website and social media platforms (Facebook and Twitter). Their website functions as a virtual library of information on trafficking in human beings, providing up-to-date news on the issues and on the activities of different national networks.

Supporting people at risk: These activities concern various forms of support provided by the networks to people considered to be potentially at risk due to their vulnerable condition, especially due to their socio-economic status. Nigeria, for example, offers scholarships for poor students and supports vulnerable families. Many of these activities are carried out for the benefit of the most vulnerable, namely women and migrant people.

The reported number of volunteers who helped Talitha Kum's activities in this area is 2,068. The respondents estimated that 215,742 persons were reached through their activities in the area of prevention.

3.2 Protection

Table 3.2 presents various activities in the area of protection of victims of human trafficking.

	Country	Lobbying and advocacy	Material support	Spiritual & psychological support	Support in judicial process	Social & workforce re-integration	No answer
Africa	Burkina Faso		x		x		
	Cameroon						x
	Ghana						x
	Kenya		x				
	Nigeria		x	x			
	South Africa		x			x	
	Tunisia		x	x	x		
	Uganda						x
	Zambia						x
	Zimbabwe		x	x		x	
	Argentina						x
	Brazil		x	x			
	Colombia						x
	Costa Rica						x
	El Salvador						x
	Guatemala						x

Region	Country						
Latin America	Honduras	x	x		x		
	Mexico		x		x		
	Nicaragua						x
	Panama						
	Paraguay						x
	Peru		x				
	Dominican Republic		x		x	x	
	Uruguay		x	x	x	x	
U.S.A. & Canada	Canada						x
	U.S.A.	x	x	x		x	
Asia	Cambodia						
	East Timor						x
	Japan	x	x	x			
	India		x			x	
	Indonesia		x				
	Korea		x	x		x	
	Myamar						x
	Malaysia						x
	Pakistan						x
	Philippines		x	x			
	Sri Lanka						x
	Thailand		x		x		
Australia and Oceania	Australia	x	x				
	New Zealand	x					
Europe	Albania						x
	Germany		x		x		
	Ireland						x
	Italy						x
	Poland						x
	Romania		x				
	Portugal						x
Total		47	5	22	8	9	7	22

Table 3.2: Activities in the area of protection

Lobbying and Advocacy: Some of the networks carry out actions aimed at influencing politics and legislation, such as petitioning the government in matters concerning trafficking in human beings, or filing appropriate paperwork on behalf of victims. The Japanese network, for example, actively supports the change in the labour law which currently exposes immigrants to the risk of exploitation. Australian network is collaborating with the government on the enactment of a law aimed at protecting the victims.

Material and economic support for survivors: These activities include assistance to survivors, relief, shelter and first aid, food, medical assistance and financial support for housing. This level of action includes work in places of exploitation, or of elevated risk of exploitation, such as border areas. Many of the victims served by the Tunisian network, for example, have been rescued from the sea. In Zimbabwe, victims have been rescued from places of exploitation. Among the main activities of material and economic support is the reception of victims in shelters, typically for a limited time necessary to achieve their rehabilitation. For example, the USA network runs several shelters that offer rehabilitation services for a period of up to one year. These services include: psychological counseling, medical services, access to continuing education, job search support, and community support.

Spiritual and psychological support: This category of services includes days of prayer, retreats and spiritual counseling for the victims, as well as moral support and companionship. The USA network for example offers retreats for survivors along with ongoing pastoral support. Different networks further provide professional psychological help to victims of trafficking. Zimbabwe offers psychological counseling and therapy and Korea is active in rehabilitation, self-sufficiency and stabilization programs for victims of sexual violence.

Legal support: These activities include legal and judicial orientation actions. Member networks report accompanying survivors to competent authorities, filing asylum request on their behalf, assisting them in judicial processes and supporting them in case of voluntary repatriation of victims.

Social and workforce reintegration: Some networks carry out actions aimed at a complete social and workforce reintegration of the victims, either in their current milieus or before voluntary repatriation. They provide education for those who want to complete their studies or technical training. South Africa, for example, offers programs in technical training aimed at equipping survivors with skills and equipment before they return to their countries of origin.

The reported number of volunteers who helped Talitha Kum's activities in this area is 1,563. The estimated number of persons that were helped through various activities in the area of protection is reported to be 39,842.

3.3 Prosecution

The area of prosecution includes: reporting of cases of human trafficking, legal assistance and support for projects aiming at rendering more effective the mechanisms of reporting of human trafficking. The activities presuppose a certain maturation of the network and are tightly related to the socio-political context of the country in which the projects are carried out.

	Country	Report and Denounce	Support victims during the judicial process	No activities
Africa	Tunisia			x
	Ghana			x
	Nigeria	x		
	Zimbabwe			x
	South Africa			x
	Kenya			x
	Burkina Faso	x		
	Cameroon			x
	Uganda			x
	Zambia			x
Latin America	Colombia			x
	Guatemala	x		
	Dominican Republic		x	
	Brazil			x
	Peru			x
	Argentina			x
	Salvador	x	x	
	Uruguay		x	
	Mexico		x	
	Paraguay			x
	Honduras		x	
	Panama			x
	Costa Rica		x	
	Nicaragua			x

U.S.A. and Canada	Canada			x
	U.S.A.		x	
Asia	Thailand	x	x	
	Pakistan			x
	Indonesia			x
	Myanmar			x
	Malaysia			x
	Japan		x	
	Cambodia			x
	Sri Lanka			x
	India	x	x	
	Philippines			x
	South Korea	x	x	
	East Timor			x
Australia and Oceania	Australia		x	
	New Zealand			x
Europe	Germany			x
	Romania		x	
	Ireland			x
	USMI Rete			x
	Albania			x
	Poland			x
	Portugal			x
Total	47	7	13	31

Table 3.3: Main activities in the area of prosecution

The majority of the networks reported no activities in this area. The report basically suggests two reasons for that: First, the networks are young or in the middle of the consolidation process and consequently focusing on prevention and protection. Second, the overall political situation in a given country may render difficult an effective cooperation with government. Some networks in predominantly Muslim countries reported this as a problem.

Report and denounce. The main activity of the networks is to report cases of human trafficking to the competent authorities. In the case of Nigeria, Burkina Faso and India, the networks denounce the traffickers so that they can be arrested. In South Korea, the victim assistance center provides shelter and protection services, and is committed to reporting instances of abuse or trafficking to civil authorities. In Thailand, specifically the network is involving in the prosecution of the fishing vessel: Assisting fishery workers in prosecuting employers with the goal of obtaining due wages and compensation.

Support victims during the judicial process. Although this activity is directly related to the level of protection, the main role of the networks in this area is to legally guide and accompany the victims in the judicial processes, particularly in the courts. The assistance can take various forms, from simple support and accompanying, counselling and therapy to providing legal services for victims. Specifically, networks in Honduras, Costa Rica, Japan, India, Australia and Romania offer legal advice, South Korea and Uruguay also bring it to the members of the network in order to they can be effective in fulfilling the objectives in the prosecution mission. Finally, Japan assists with financial aid and translators to the victims during the judicial processes.

Most of the networks are involved in the prevention, protection and association activities and not so much on rendering effective the mechanisms of reporting of human trafficking. For comparison purposes: 81 activities were mentioned in the area of prevention, compared to 20 in the area of prosecution. Seven of them are directly related to the reporting of victims to the authorities, the other 13 are associated with supporting victims in the prosecution processes.

An interesting fact is that only certain number of networks in Africa (2), Asia (3) and Latin America (2) are involved in reporting cases to law enforcement authorities. Overall, there are but a few countries where these activities take place. Probably the contexts of departure represent more risks for the victims and for the complainants. Another factor could be that the networks are still in a process of consolidation, focusing on activities that are more immediate and require less legal expertise. The case of the United States, Canada,

Australia, New Zealand and Europe as places of transit and arrival should be carefully studied. Maybe for these networks it is a better option to be involved in the lobbying and advocacy activities than in the area of prosecution.

By definition, effective prosecution of cases of human trafficking presupposes a certain level of institutional and political development. An NGO or a faith-based initiative cannot accomplish it on its own. A functioning system of law enforcement and administration of justice as well as a general culture that encourages cooperation between state and civil society are needed. In absence of these, probably it is more effective for the religious to dedicate their resources to prevention and protection.

With regard to Talitha Kum's actions in the area of prosecution, countries can roughly be classified into three groups. First, those lacking an effective institutional framework an/or a political culture that encourages cooperation between state and faith-based organization. In these conditions, Talitha Kum's initiatives would be either ineffective or risky. Second, countries with a reasonable developed system of law enforcement and administration of justice and with a political climate that makes cooperation possible. Third, countries with mature and effective institutions capable of detecting and prosecuting offenders. Here, network's role is quite limited and can even be superfluous.

The reported number of volunteers who helped Talitha Kum's activities in this area is 254. The respondents estimated that 5,141 victims of human trafficking were helped, directly or indirectly, through their activities in the area of prosecution.

3.4 Partnership

The initiatives aimed at strengthening partnerships and coordination occur through networks' participation with other agencies. The main activities at this level are the attendance at significant meetings (either for the members of the network or with other organizations), organization of various awareness and prevention activities, protection of victims, interventions with governments and administrative organs with the aim of promoting better laws and their implementation and the financing of the networks.

The cooperative work has been carried out with various institutions. Among the main organizations are: governmental agencies in all three branches of government as well as various agencies; NGOs; Catholic and non-Catholic religious institutions as well as individuals. This cooperation occurs at the local, regional and international level. We will explain the details of each activity as follows.

	Country	Networking at meetings	Joint actions w/ other institutions	Financing	Nothing
Africa	Tunisia	x	x		
	Ghana	x			
	Nigeria	x	x		
	Zimbabwe				x
	South Africa	x			
	Kenya	x	x		
	Burkina Faso				x
	Cameroon				x
	Uganda				x
	Zambia				x
	Colombia		x		
	Guatemala	x			
	Dominican Republic	x			
	Brazil	x	x	x	
	Peru		x		
	Argentina				x

Region	Country					
Latin America	Salvador					x
	Uruguay					x
	Mexico			x		
	Paraguay					x
	Honduras		x			
	Panama					x
	Costa Rica		x	x		
	Nicaragua			x		
U.S.A. & Canada	Canada			x		
	U.S.A.			x		
Asia	Thailand		x			
	Pakistan		x	x		
	Indonesia			x		
	Myanmar					x
	Malaysia					x
	Japan			x		
	Cambodia					x
	Sri Lanka					x
	India				x	
	Philippines		x			
	South Korea		x			
	South East Asia					x
	East Timor			x		
Australia & Oceania	Australia			x		
	New Zealand			x		
Europe	Germany		x			
	Romania		x			
	Ireland					x
	USMI Rete			x		
	Albania					x
	Poland					x
Total		47	16	18	2	20

Table 3.4: Main activities in the area of partnership

Nineteen networks reported no activities in this area. Only Tunisia's network provided a reason for the lack of partnership with institutions, namely the inability to establish links with the government because of the political climate in the country. They team up with individual collaborators instead.

Networking through meetings. Holding meetings is one of the activities that makes cooperation with other institutions stronger. Generally, their objective is the formation of the members of the network as well as sharing information. For example, Brazil's network conducts frequent training meetings at international, regional and local levels. Honduras promotes meetings for border pastoral agents. In Mexico, Costa Rica, Honduras and the Philippines the networks carry out workshops and seminars with the participation of some international agencies, such as OSCE (Organization for Security and Co-operation in Europe). Germany, Kenya and South Korea also emphasize the importance of holding international conferences and organising a World Congress on the issue. We provide some examples of such activities.

The congress "Borders are not barriers" is an example of continental cooperation. It was organized by USCSAHT in Cleveland, Ohio, in October 2018. Representatives of the Canadian network, Rahamin Network, Red Rama, Dominican Republic Network, Red Taw, Red Kawsay, and Um Grito Pela Vida attended, in total sixty-one people, including representatives from all networks in the Western Hemisphere as well as the Talitha Kum international coordinator.

Most networks around the world have established links with government offices and agencies in their respective countries. For example, South Africa participates in several regional meetings sponsored by the government. The Ghana network meets regionally with the government welfare, migration and forced labour department. In Pakistan, the network develops collaborative work with the national as well as local governments.

Meetings with government representatives and institutions are geared towards the consultation and enactment of specific laws, or serve to report certain crimes. New Zealand urged the government to pass an anti-slavery act modelled on a U.K. law. In the Dominican Republic, the network works with the government towards establishing an action plan against human trafficking, as well as with the attorney general and workers of the Ministry of Women with the purpose of effecting specific changes of the existing laws. Talitha Peru designed and implemented regional or zonal action plans with the Government. In South Korea, members of the network participate in public hearings of the government to express their position with regard to women's rights. The networks have also held working sessions with the government in Australia and India.

However, inter-institutional work does not end with the government. Most networks seek to engage ecclesial organizations and offices, e.g., religious communities, parishes, women's groups, Catholic educational institutions, and bishops. For example, the Nigerian network is involved in many projects with religious communities and NGOs. In Guatemala, the network works in close coordination with the Episcopal Conference and the Office of the Procurator of the Nation to prepare materials, plan and evaluate activities.

Awareness raising, promotion, prevention, and protection of victims. Many organizations that work together share information, raise awareness of this social problem, and try to put in place effective prevention. Mexico and Pakistan have established partnerships with universities aimed at initiating training and prevention programs with student communities. The network in Nigeria, in collaboration with local institutions and parishes, held prayer events, vigils, educational programs and the celebration of the World Day of Prayer and Awareness Against Human Trafficking (February 8th).

The links established with other institutions have strengthened the material, legal, psychological and spiritual assistance to the victims. For example, Tunisia's network works with a group of doctors to secure medical treatment for migrants. At the same time, they also have recruited legal help to defend migrants detained in jail. The network in Japan with the cooperation of some religious communities and dioceses has offered refuge to the victims. In Australia, there is a project with a large Catholic hospital system to educate frontline staff about indicators of human trafficking, and to assist procurement officers in investigating the supply chain for signs of slavery so that the latter can be eliminated. Furthermore, the network works with NGOs, including the Red Cross, in a network of response to trafficking in people in Sydney.

Financing. Financing is an important collaborative task that or recent years has begun to take on some urgency. Brazil has the help of several international agencies that finance their projects: Adveniat, Arise, Verapaz, and Miserior. The Indian network is also involved in this area.

The activities carried out in the area of partnership show that it is impossible to effectively help to prevent, protect and denounce the victims of human trafficking if the networks are functioning as islands. This form of synergy includes not only Catholic or religious institutions but also the government and its agencies, as well as other types of groups and people interested in this field.

Although collaborative work continues to grow, it remains a challenge in Africa, Asia and Latin America. The first step towards partnership involves participating in local, national or international meetings. Networks also underline the need to work collaboratively to effectively protect and assist the victims. In addition to this, partnership could also contribute to the economic sustainability of the networks. However, the largely volunteer character of networks and technical difficulties at maintaining a stable and effective communication remain obstacles to effective collaboration.

The nature of institutions that work in partnership with our networks is difficult to specify. Several respondents refer to them only in the most generic fashion, such as "institutions" or "organizations" without indicating their names. However, we can infer the following conclusions. Local or national governments, including their law enforcement and judicial agencies, as well as a large number of Catholic institutions (conferences of bishops, Caritas and religious communities) are the main allies of Talitha Kum throughout the world.

In Africa, our networks partner preferably with governments, Catholic institutions and NGOs. Latin American networks work mostly with religious organizations, regional Talitha networks and various government institutions. In Asia, national networks develop activities with international organizations and various ecclesial institutions. In Oceania the great allies are governments and civil NGOs. Finally, in Europe and the USA, effective relations have been established with the regional Talitha networks.

The respondents indicated that nearly 900 sisters and Talitha Kum volunteers participated in activities related to partnership. An estimated 12,000 persons were involved in these activities.

3.5 How can Talitha Kum make your work more effective?

In the last section of the questionnaire, network representatives were asked to identify some areas where the global network might help. Their responses were summarised into four categories: finances, material and informational support, formation and meetings, and promotion and cooperation.

	Country	Financial support	Material support & information	Meetings & formation	Promotion & cooperation	No answer
Africa	Burkina Faso		x	x		
	Cameroon					x
	Ghana	x				
	Kenya	x				
	Nigeria				x	
	South Africa				x	
	Tunisia	x		x		
	Uganda					x
	Zambia		x	x		
	Zimbabwe	x				
Latin America	Argentina		x	x	x	
	Brazil	x		x	x	
	Colombia			x		
	Costa Rica		x	x	x	
	El Salvador		x			
	Guatemala			x		
	Honduras		x			
	Mexico					x
	Nicaragua			x		
	Panama					x
	Paraguay		x			
	Peru		x	x		
	Dominican Republic		x			
	Uruguay	x		x		

Region	Country					
U.S.A and Canada	Canada					x
	U.S.A.		x			
Asia	Cambodia					x
	East Timor	x				
	Japan		x	x		
	India		x		x	
	Indonesia	x		x		
	Korea				x	
	Myanmar	x			x	
	Malaysia					x
	Pakistan				x	
	Philippines			x	x	
	Sri Lanka		x			
	Thailand		x		x	
Australia & Oceania	Australia		x		x	
	New Zealand		x			
Europe	Albania					x
	Germany		x			
	Ireland					x
	Italy					
	Poland	x	x			
	Romania	x			x	
	Portugal					x
Total	**47**	**11**	**18**	**14**	**13**	**10**

Table 3.5: How can Talitha Kum International support your work?

Financing. Economic support was one of the main requests to Talitha Kum. The main needs identified by networks include: construction of housing structures that will serve as a refuge for the survivors; setting up of offices for coordination; and funds for salaries of employees and administrative staff.

Support material and information. This category mainly refers to the material and content of animation, and information and knowledge as a support for the formation of network members but also as an aid in the various educational activities and laboratories they offer. The networks require information and up-to-date facts on the issue of trafficking, strategies to combat it as well as sharing the experiences of other networks. Some of them ask for a more accessible and easier form of communication, particularly with reference to the website. Another aspect of this category refers to the request for a guide for technological and IT support.

Strengthening of networks through regular meetings. Many networks ask for meetings and training sessions about the reality of human trafficking and about strategies that will enable them to operate in their specific contexts. Meetings are important for strengthening the communion of networks at international and local level through the sharing of experiences and opinions among members.

Promotion and collaboration. The networks wish for a precise intervention by Talitha Kum aimed at boosting the visibility of their work. This could take the form of informing and mobilising member communities and major superiors of religious organizations as well as civil organizations, and lead to greater collaboration and cooperation in the fight against trafficking. The need for integrating laity into these activities was also mentioned.

3.6 When you think of the near future (3-5 years), what are the most significant challenges that you will need to address?

Respondents were further asked to identify significant challenges that they foresee in the near future. The answers ranged from obtaining sufficient personnel and material resources to challenges inherent in the challenging political and cultural environment in which they operate. Formation of both the general public and those on the frontlines of intervention was also mentioned.

	Country	Material & financial resources	Collaboration & active participation	Formation & awareness raising	Bureaucracy & corruption	Relations w/ governments	No answer
Africa	Burkina Faso	x	x				
	Cameroon						x
	Ghana			x			
	Kenya	x		x			
	Nigeria	x					
	South Africa			x			
	Tunisia			x		x	
	Uganda						x
	Zambia						x
	Zimbabwe	x					
Latin America	Argentina		x	x			
	Brazil	x	x		x		
	Colombia	x		x			
	Costa Rica	x	x				
	El Salvador	x	x			x	
	Guatemala		x	x		x	
	Honduras		x	x			
	Mexico		x	x	x	x	
	Nicaragua		x	x			
	Panama						x

Region	Country						
	Paraguay			x			
	Peru		x	x			
	Dominican Republic		x			x	
	Uruguay	x	x	x		x	
U.S.A. & Canada	Canada						x
	U.S.A.	x	x	x			
Asia	Cambodia						x
	East Timor		x				
	Japan		x				
	India		x		x		
	Indonesia				x		
	Korea					x	
	Myamar	x	x	x			
	Malaysia						x
	Pakistan		x				
	Philippines						x
	Sri Lanka	x	x	x		x	
	Thailand	x	x				
Australia & Oceania	Australia	x		x			
	New Zealand			x		x	
Europe	Albania						x
	Germany			x			
	Ireland						x
	Italy			x			
	Poland						x
	Romania		x				
	Portugal						x
Total	**46**	**14**	**20**	**20**	**5**	**9**	**12**

Table 3.6: Most important challenges in the near to medium future

Material and financial resources. One of the important challenges that the networks feel they are facing is providing for economic sustainability of their work. They are concerned about maintaining the existing funding and obtaining new one for the various projects, in particular educational and work opportunities for the most vulnerable. Many have expressed the need for suitable shelters for victims.

Collaboration and active participation. Different networks identified the indifference or low level of involvement by consecrated persons and ecclesial leaders as one of the major challenges. At the same time, there is a need for a more articulated collaboration within the individual networks, at regional and continental level, along the chain of the trafficking that includes places of origin, transit and destination of victims. Finally, collaboration with government agencies and civil society remains a pressing need.

Formation and awareness raising. Another important challenge is the training of network collaborators. That includes professional training that will enable them to adequately support survivors, and knowledge of relevant strategies to address the issue in their own context. Solid training and awareness-raising campaigns are necessary for effective social and political action.

Bureaucracy and corruption. Several Latin American and Asian networks identified corruption, violence, injustice, manipulation of laws and slow administrative and bureaucratic action as significant challenges in their activities.

Collaboration with government and law enforcement. An important challenge regards the strengthening of the synergy with government organizations to counter this crime. This synergy is crucial when effective legislative action and implementation of relevant laws is concerned.

3.7 Looking back at your work, which were your most significant accomplishments?

This question provides insight into networks' own perception of its effectiveness. One can assume that respondents will indicate those activities that they found significant, meaningful and effective. The analysis of their responses will provide a qualitative measure of Talitha Kum's performance and will focus its future allocation of resources.

	Country	Protection & assistance of victims	Awareness & prevention	Creation & strengthening of the network	Partnership	No answer
Africa	Tunisia	x				
	Ghana		x			
	Nigeria		x			
	Zimbabwe		x	x		
	South Africa					x
	Kenya		x			
	Burkina Faso	x	x	x		
	Cameroon			x		
	Uganda					x
	Zambia			x		
Latin America	Colombia	x				
	Guatemala		x	x	x	
	Dominican Republic	x			x	
	Brazil	x	x			
	Peru			x	x	
	Argentina			x		
	Salvador		x		x	
	Uruguay	x	x		x	
	Mexico	x		x		
	Paraguay					x
	Honduras			x		

Region	Country					
	Panama					x
	Costa Rica		x	x	x	
	Nicaragua	x	x			
U.S.A. & Canada	Canada					x
	U.S.A.		x	x	x	
Asia	Thailand					
	Pakistan	x	x		x	
	Indonesia		x			
	Myanmar					x
	Malaysia					x
	Japan	x				
	Cambodia					x
	Sri Lanka		x	x	x	
	India			x		
	Philippines					x
	South Korea					x
	East Timor		x			
Australia & Oceania	Australia	x				
	New Zealand				x	
Europe	Germany	x				
	Romania					x
	Ireland					x
	USMI Rete			x	x	
	Albania					x
	Poland					x
	Portugal					x
Total	**47**	**12**	**16**	**14**	**11**	**15**

Table 3.7: Significant accomplishments

Protection and assistance of victims. A comprehensive assistance to victims of human trafficking features as one of the most important achievements of the networks. This goal comprises diverse actions such as: educational projects with the victims, carried out particularly in Tunisia, Burkina Faso and Colombia; material support, for example the Dominican Republic and Brazil; and shelters, as in Mexico, Nicaragua, Pakistan and Japan.

Promotion of awareness and protection are seen as vital to overall mission of Talitha Kum. Public celebrations in Ghana and Nigeria have helped achieve this goal. In these two countries the celebration of February 8th has involved many people. Zimbabwe, Kenya, Burkina Faso, Brazil, Salvador all look positively upon the activities they conducted in educational institutions. In Uruguay, Pakistan, Indonesia, Sri Lanka, East Timor, successful awareness days have been held. The networks of Guatemala and the USA use the media as an effective instrument to raise awareness of this problem, as well as to grow and strengthen the network. Uruguay, the Dominican Republic and Australia greatly value the enactment or modification of laws that protect the rights of victims and of those who help them.

Setting-up and strengthening of the network. Although some networks have only recently started their work, they themselves highlight their progress and the strengthening of their work. USCSAHT believes that its strong presence in social networks has strengthened the network and contributed to its growth. Zimbabwe appreciates the visit of the Talitha Kum global coordinator, while Mexico and Sri Lanka appreciate the help of the international team. Peru and Argentina have advanced with the creation of regional networks and the strengthening of the national team. The networks in India, Burkina Faso, Cameroon, Uganda, Zambia, Costa Rica and USMI affirm the value of international conferences and meetings as an important means for the formation and strengthening of the network worldwide.

Partnership. One of the most important conclusions is the need to continue working in collaboration with other institutions. Guatemala particularly appreciates the activities carried out with the help of religious congregations, schools and universities. The ties established with governments and their agencies have been vital for the enactment of certain laws and the elaboration of many action plans. This is the case of the Dominican Republic, Peru, Uruguay, Costa Rica, Pakistan and Sri Lanka. In New Zealand, the government has attended the meetings of the network. Another important link is established with Catholic institutions: bishops' conferences, as in the case of the Peru network; and others such as the Coalition of Catholic Organizations against Trafficking in Persons (CCOAHT); the National Association of Catholic Education (NCEA); the National Conference of Catholic Women (NCCW); and the Leadership Conference of Women Religious (LCWR) in USA. USCSAHT is actively networking with a variety of ecclesial organizations.

3.8 Conclusion

The main activities of networks fall into the areas of prevention and protection. The data does not show significant differences between continents in this regard. As far as prevention is concerned, the pre-eminent actions concern training and awareness of the issue of trafficking. With reference to protection, the actions that prevail are those referring to the material assistance of the victims. Most networks are involved in offering material support, shelter, food, and medical care to survivors.

The activities that concern direct influence on politics and legislation, lobbying and advocacy, are the least common among the networks, and there are notable differences between the continents. Those that have the greatest impact are the USA and Oceania, while the other countries, with few exceptions, did not report activities in this category. This apparent lack of action could be due to the fact that many networks are in the consolidation stages, or to specific local political and social factors.

In the area of prosecution, about 40 percent of networks indicated two types of activities: reporting cases of trafficking to competent authorities, and legal assistance to victims. The latter is characteristic of Latin America and Asia, less of Africa and Europe.

Lastly, in the area of partnership, two types of activities were mentioned by respondents, namely networking and protection of victims. It is obvious that, given the international nature of the crime, partnering across political jurisdictions is key to successful action and for a more effective protection of victims. A second type of partnering involves various organizations within individual states, as cooperation between heterogeneous actors (e.g., state and civil society, religious and non-religious, etc.) is needed in order to effectively combat the phenomenon.

Part IV: Comparative analysis
of data collected in 2015 and 2018

Sr. Gabriella Bottani, SMC | Peter Lah S.J.

The time framework 2015 – 2018 object of the analyses presented here coincides with the change in leadership at the International Coordination Office at the UISG in Rome. During the first period of Talitha Kum, from its foundation in 2009 through 2015, the main activities of the International Office in Rome were focused on formation and on setting-up of networks in various parts of the world. Since 2015, Talitha Kum identified the need to widen its networking ability beyond the national to the regional, continental and global level.

The data collected in 2015 provided important input to the participants at the Second International Coordination Committee, gathered in Rome in January 2016. They were tasked with setting priorities for the future of Talitha Kum and proposed the following four:

- **NETWORKING**: To promote the cooperation and the connection between religious congregations, facilitating networking at the regional and continental levels, in collaboration with other governmental and non-governmental organizations.
- **COMMUNICATION:** To organize data collection from networks members, in order to maximize communication, and the exchange of information, of data and of good practices.
- **FORMATION:** To create courses, workshops and seminars aimed at promoting:
  o The qualification of the members of Talitha Kum, in the service of leadership;
  o The formation and strengthening of Talitha Kum networks, offering the Talitha Kum courses dedicated to the professional development of those who want to combat trafficking, accompany victims, and work toward their reintegration into society.

- **GEOGRAPHICAL SCOPE**: To give priority to Africa and the Middle East, regions where the phenomenon of trafficking is growing. To step up efforts in the areas of prevention, protection and assistance to the victims of trafficking.

The data collected in 2015 presented a very differentiated reality. Some Networks were limited to the nation in which they were based, whereas others were multi-national, even continental wide – such was the case of Europe.

The comparison of the data collected in 2015 and in 2018, respectively, highlights the development of the Talitha Kum's networks in the time framework of three years.

To organize better the data in 2018, the team in charge of creating the database decided to implement better identification of the different level of networking and the interconnectedness among the different levels. At the same time, the National Network was selected *as the basic unit* for the data collection.

In 2018 we witnessed a slight increase in the response rate, from 84 percent to 86 percent in 2015. This was achieved by using various channels of communication and by follow-up soliciting in cases where there was no immediate response. We believe the high response rate to be an indicator of commitment and belonging to the core mission of Talitha Kum.

The 2018 phase of data collection, using different questionnaires for National and Regional/Continental levels was able to make a better distinction between two different levels of networking:

- the grouping of networks at regional level: like Red Ramà in Central America or Talitha Kum South East Asia.
- the subgrouping inside the same country, like in Brazil, India or Indonesia.

In 2018 the Regional Networks in Latin America and Asia were able to implement nine networks, representing almost all the countries involved in the regional networks. This influenced significantly the growing of the Talitha Kum Networks, without a corresponding growing of the number of the countries.

This indicate not only a quantitative growing of the number but also a qualitative element, mainly in their capacity to network and in the identity of Talitha Kum. Talitha Kum Networks are in fact grass-roots oriented, inter-congregational and under the responsibility of the respective Conferences of Major Superior.

In the intervening years between the two surveys, two networks ceased to operate (the Netherlands, Zambia), while eleven new national networks were founded.

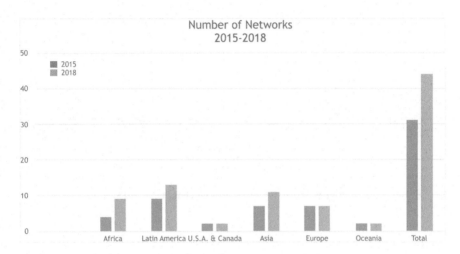

Figure 4.1: The Number of the Networks
of Talitha Kum in 2015 and 2018, by Continent

During the same period seventeen networks were able to expand their organization in 124 subgroups. Their size and complexity is uneven (the median number of subgroups per network is five). This indicates that a few networks in big countries like Brazil and India have a great numbers of subgroups, while the majority have only few.

In 2018 three new regional/continental networks where registered: one in Oceania and one in Latin America. Their intent is to coordinate the networking at the continental level and to expand the creation of new networks in other countries of the region. The regional network in Asia aims to facilitate the expansion of networking capacity in East Asia.

The quantitative growth of Talitha Kum Networks at the national and regional levels coincided with a significant improvement of anti-trafficking activities in the areas of Prevention, Protection, Prosecution and Partnership. In subsequent paragraphs we are discussing the development of Talitha Kum's activities in the period 2015-2018.

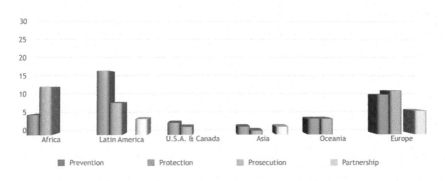

Figure 4.2: activities by area and continent, 2015

Prevention

Prevention activities were indicated by the largest number of national networks, both in 2015 (25 countries) and 2018 (34 countries). The main activities are to raise awareness through formation and educational activities. Social Media Campaigns have increased slightly in this period. While in 2015 the National Networks reported activities in area of research as prevention strategy, in 2018 several activities aimed at helping people at risk to be trafficked were introduced. This can be seen as indicator of specialization and differentiation of prevention activities to better suit specific target groups.

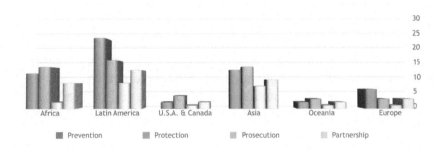

Figure 4.3: activities by area and continent, 2018

Protection

About 50% of the Network of Talitha Kum reported that they provided services to survivors. The comparative analysis of data highlights a slight growth of the number of National Networks and the inclusion in 2018 of a further level of services aimed at social rehabilitation and reintegration of survivors. A different trend, instead, is observed in advocacy and lobbying activities which decreased from 11 to 5 countries.

Prosecution

Prosecution activities were not reported in 2015, some of them most likely converged in juridical services provided to survivors. Nevertheless the inclusion in 2018 of activities of reporting, denouncing, offering support throughout the juridical process, show a significant qualitative growth of Talitha Kum Networks in this area of services.

Partnership

The graphic shows clearly the increased ability to connect with other organizations. In 2015 the Networks reported a great number of activities "ad intra", necessary for the building up of the Talitha Kum Networks. During the three years the National Networks expanded their partnership efforts, namely: participating/organizing meeting with other organizations, setting up partnership and collaboration for the implementation of joint actions and fundraising. All this indicates an increase in visibility and recognition of Talitha Kum Networks in the world.

All the indicators show a general growth of networking capacity in quantitative as well in qualitative aspects, such as: increase in membership, better collaboration skills, more sharing and last but not least better collaboration in the implementation of anti-trafficking activities.

Chiesa e Società 4

PONTIFICIA
UNIVERSITÀ
GREGORIANA